Hal Leonard *More* Easy Songs for Ukulele

UKULELE METHOD
Supplement to Any Ukulele Method

Play the Melodies and Chords of
20 Pop, Rock, Country, Folk and Blues Songs

Book
ISBN 978-1-4803-3992-7

Book/Audio
ISBN 978-1-4803-3991-0

T0084245

Visit Hal Leonard Online at
www.halleonard.com

Contact us:
Hal Leonard
7777 West Bluemound Road
Milwaukee, WI 53213
Email: info@halleonard.com

In Europe, contact:
Hal Leonard Europe Limited
42 Wigmore Street
Marylebone, London, W1U 2RN
Email: info@halleonardeurope.com

In Australia, contact:
Hal Leonard Australia Pty. Ltd.
4 Lentara Court
Cheltenham, Victoria, 3192 Australia
Email: info@halleonard.com.au

Gentle On My Mind

Words and Music by
JOHN HARTFORD

Verse

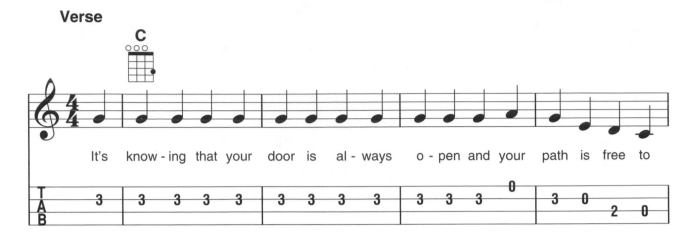

It's know-ing that your door is al-ways o-pen and your path is free to

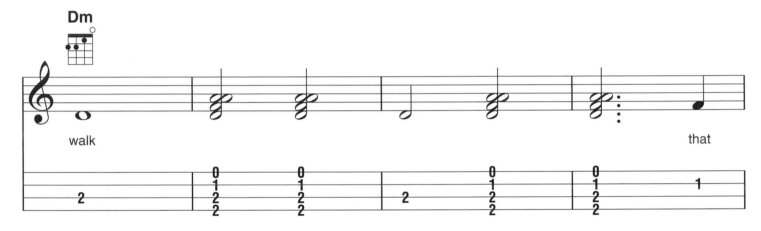

walk that

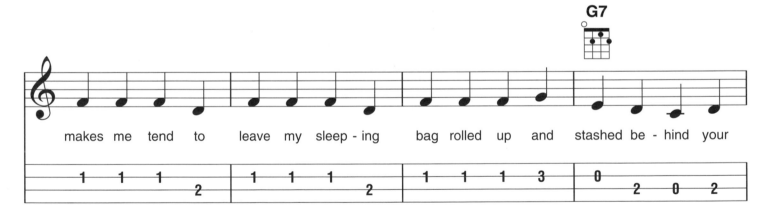

makes me tend to leave my sleep-ing bag rolled up and stashed be-hind your

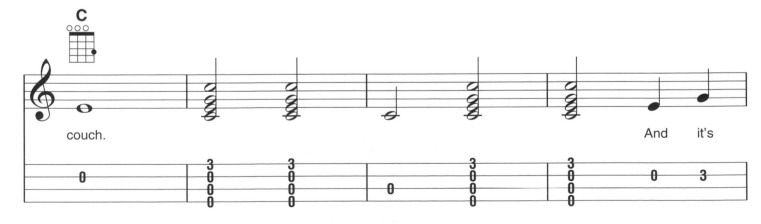

couch. And it's

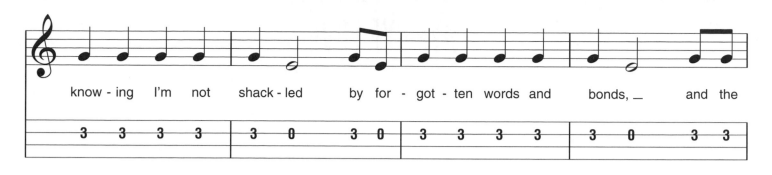

know - ing I'm not shack - led by for - got - ten words and bonds, ___ and the

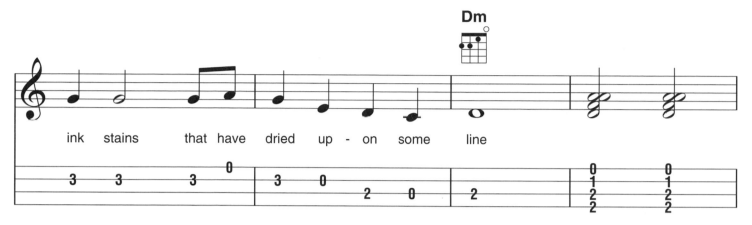

ink stains that have dried up - on some line

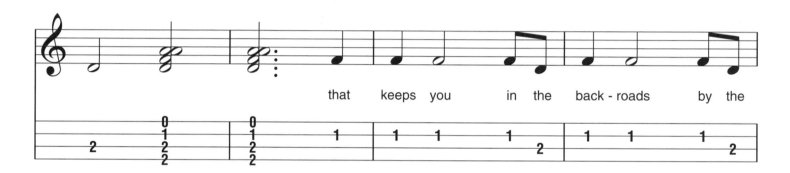

that keeps you in the back - roads by the

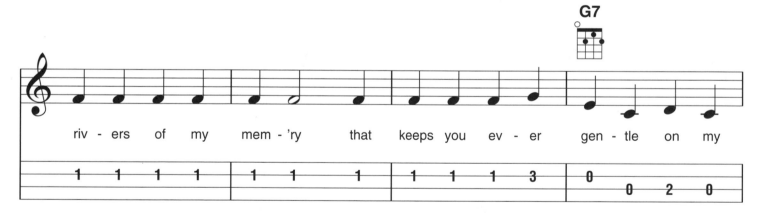

riv - ers of my mem - 'ry that keeps you ev - er gen - tle on my

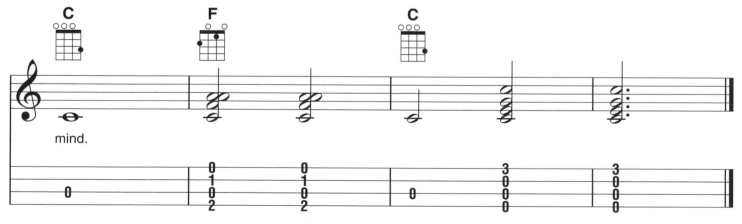

mind.

BYE BYE LOVE

Words and Music by FELICE BRYANT
and BOUDLEAUX BRYANT

Verse

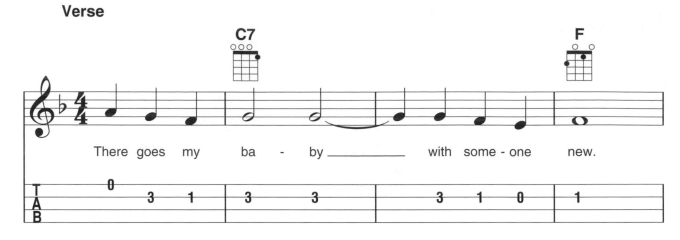

There goes my ba - by _____ with some - one new.

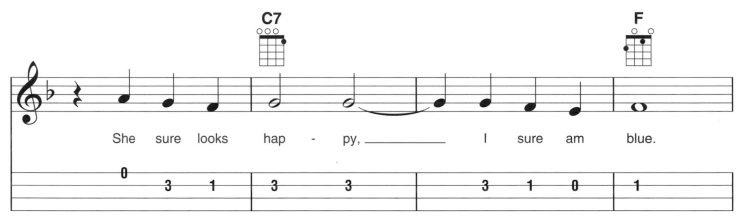

She sure looks hap - py, _____ I sure am blue.

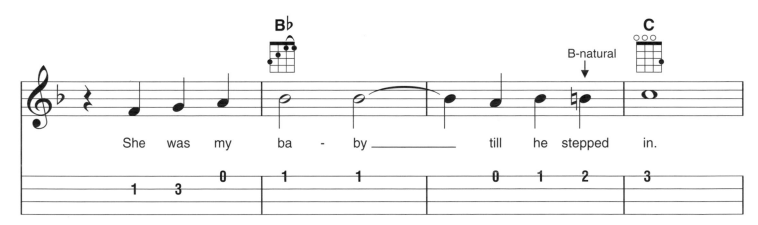

She was my ba - by _____ till he stepped in.

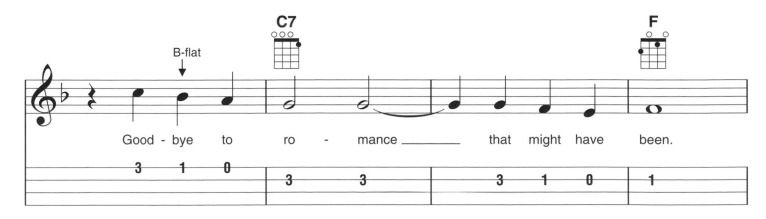

Good - bye to ro - mance _____ that might have been.

BLOWIN' IN THE WIND

Words and Music by
BOB DYLAN

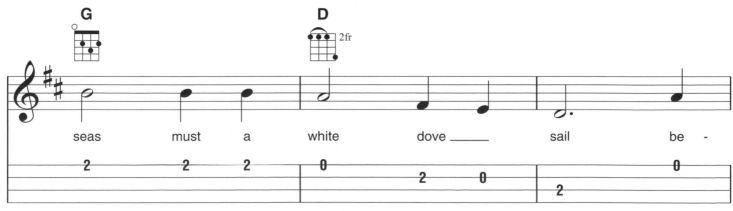

As Tears Go By

Words and Music by MICK JAGGER,
KEITH RICHARDS and ANDREW LOOG OLDHAM

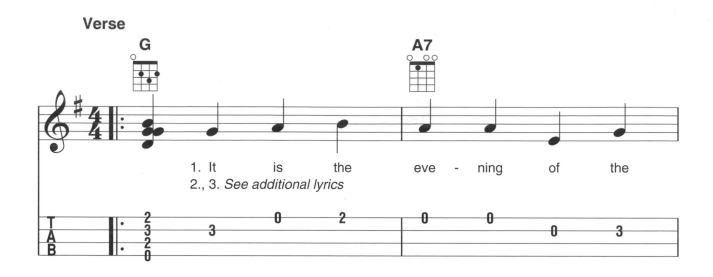

1. It is the eve - ning of the
2., 3. See additional lyrics

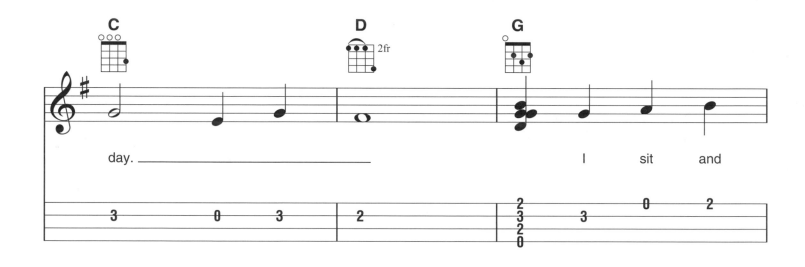

day. _____ I sit and

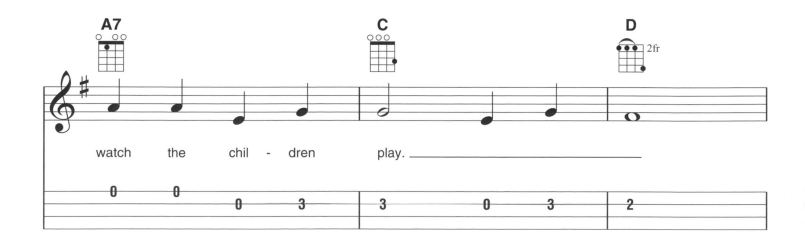

watch the chil - dren play. _____

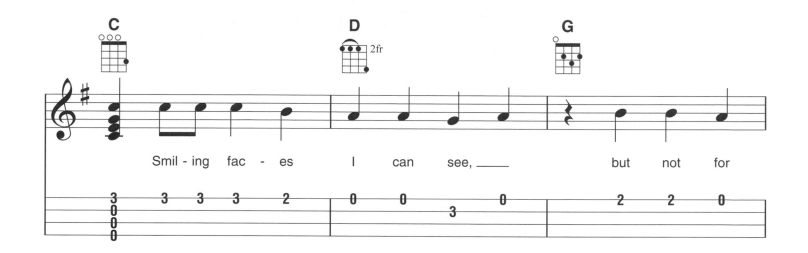

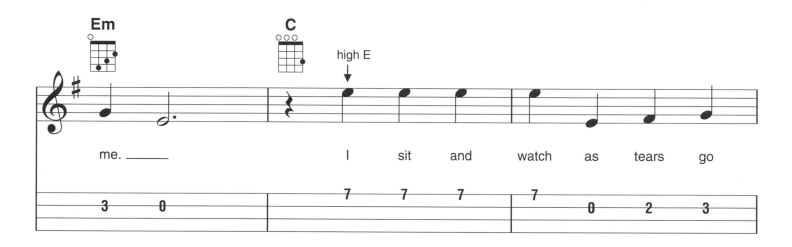

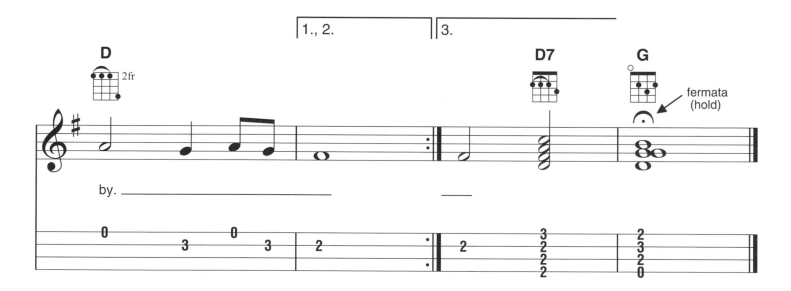

Additional Lyrics

2. My riches can't buy everything.
   I want to hear the children sing.
   All I hear is the sound of rain falling on the ground.
   I sit and watch as tears go by.

3. It is the evening of the day.
   I sit and watch the children play,
   Doing things I used to do they think are new.
   I sit and watch as tears go by.

I'D LIKE TO TEACH THE WORLD TO SING

Words and Music by BILL BACKER,
ROQUEL DAVIS, ROGER COOK
and ROGER GREENAWAY

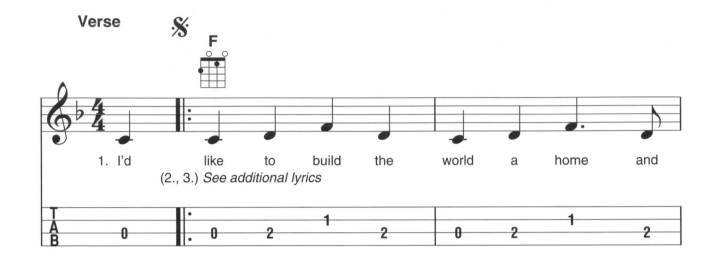

1. I'd like to build the world a home and
(2., 3.) *See additional lyrics*

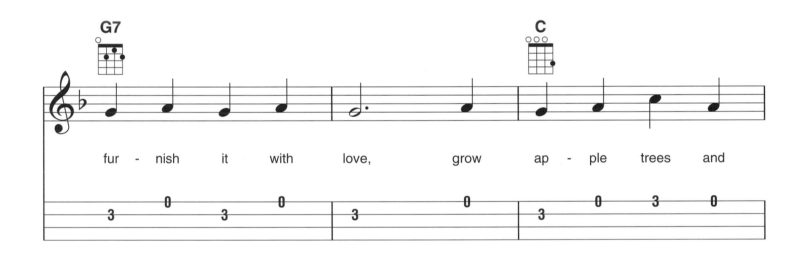

fur - nish it with love, grow ap - ple trees and

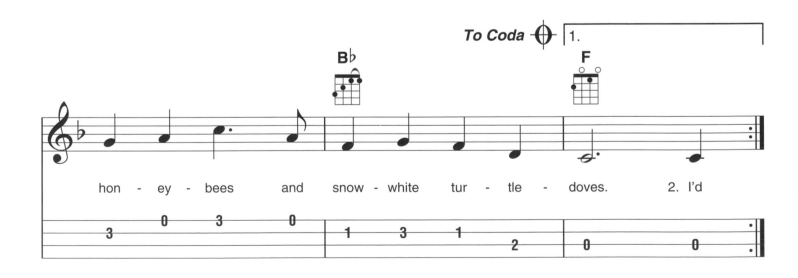

hon - ey - bees and snow - white tur - tle - doves. 2. I'd

Additional Lyrics

2. I'd like to teach the world to sing in perfect harmony.
   I'd like to hold it in my arms and keep it company.

3. I'd like to see the world, for once, all standing hand in hand,
   And hear them echo through the hills for peace throughout the land.

FIELDS OF GOLD

Music and Lyrics by
STING

Verse

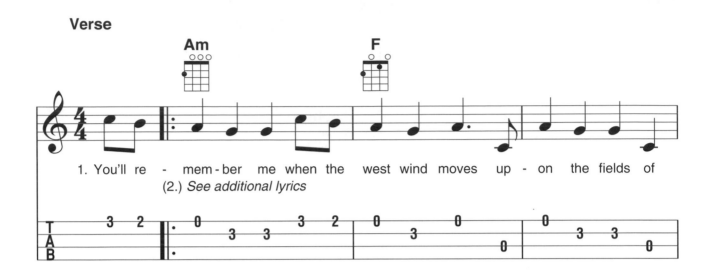

1. You'll re - mem - ber me when the west wind moves up - on the fields of
(2.) *See additional lyrics*

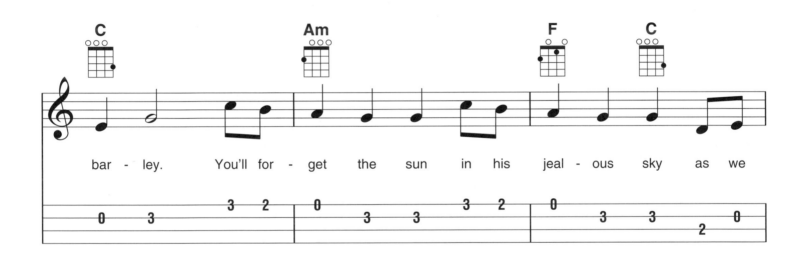

bar - ley. You'll for - get the sun in his jeal - ous sky as we

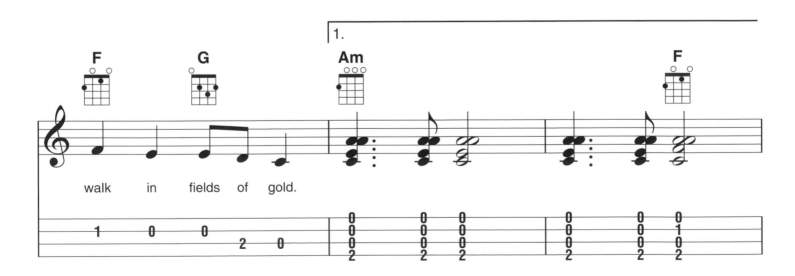

walk in fields of gold.

Additional Lyrics

2. So she took her love for to gaze a while
   Upon the fields of barley.
   In his arms she fell as her hair came down
   Among the fields of gold.

IF YOU COULD READ MY MIND

Words and Music by
GORDON LIGHTFOOT

Verse

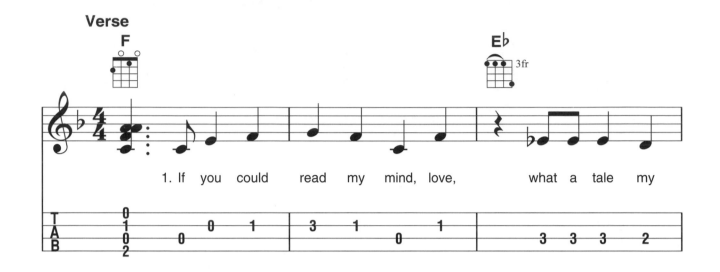

1. If you could read my mind, love, what a tale my

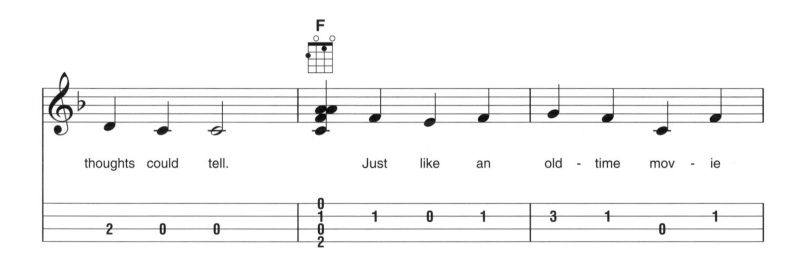

thoughts could tell. Just like an old-time mov-ie

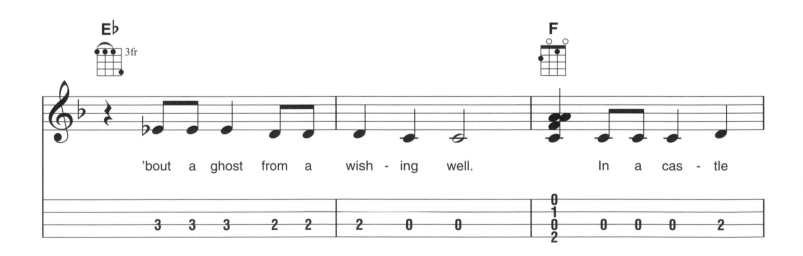

'bout a ghost from a wish-ing well. In a cas-tle

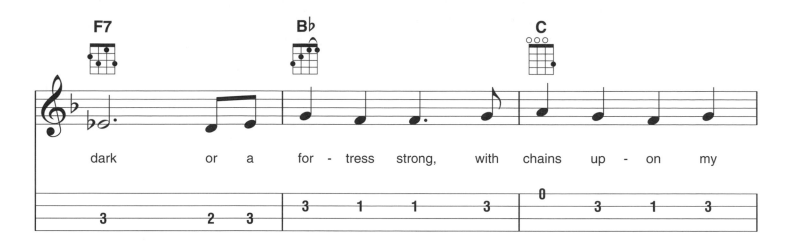

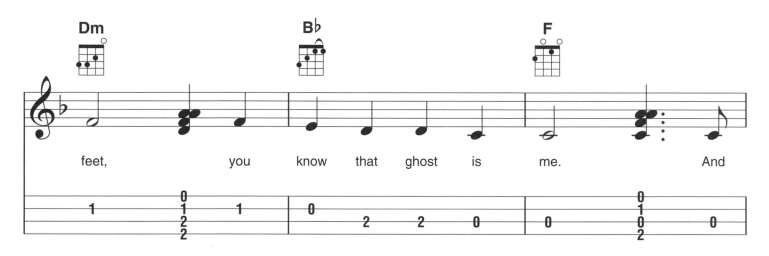

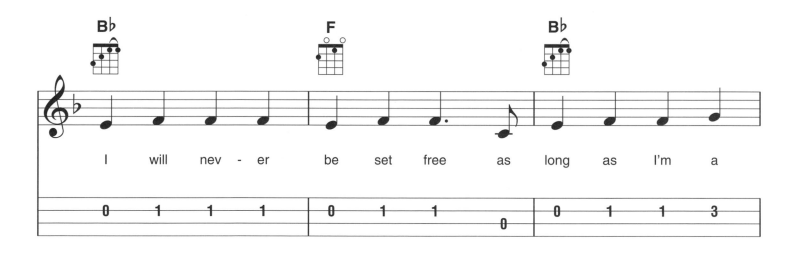

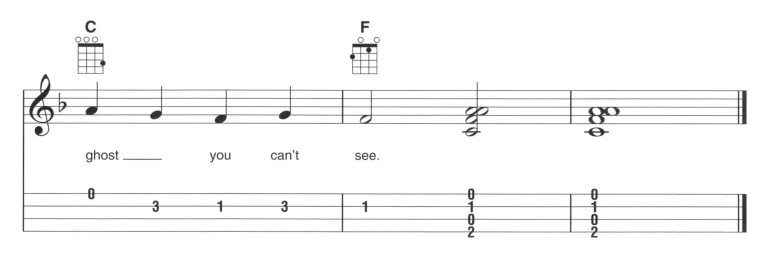

SHOWER THE PEOPLE

Words and Music by
JAMES TAYLOR

Verse

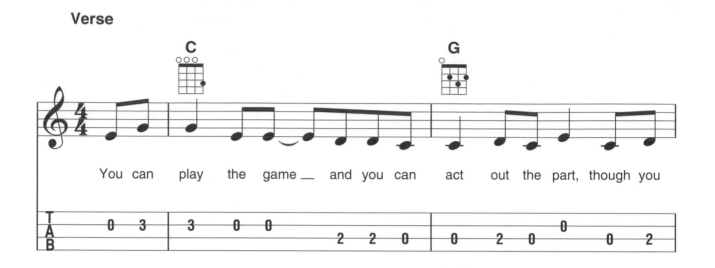

You can play the game __ and you can act out the part, though you

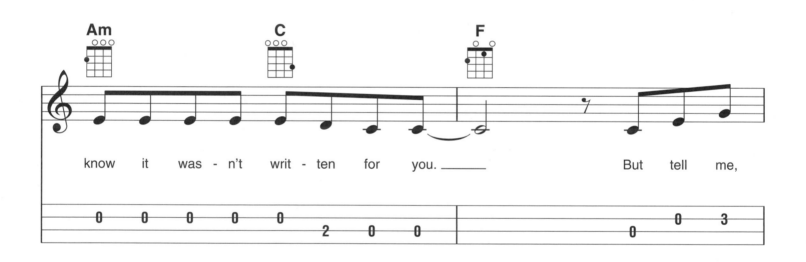

know it was-n't writ-ten for you. _____ But tell me,

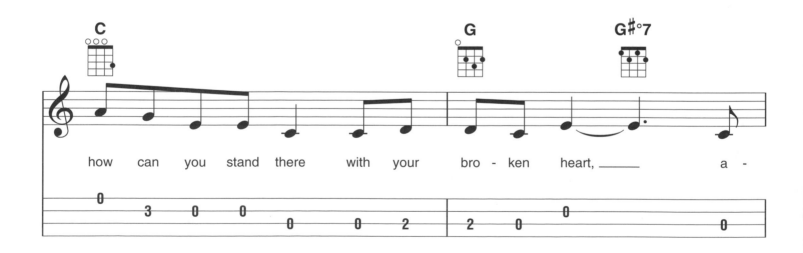

how can you stand there with your bro-ken heart, _____ a-

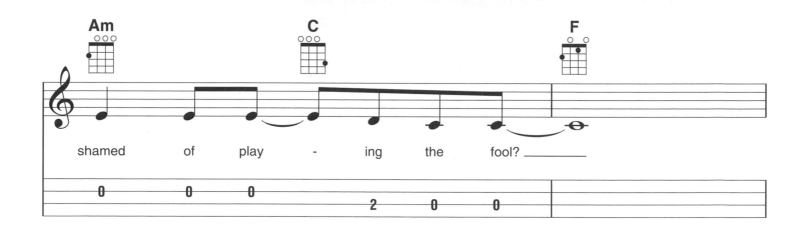

shamed of play - ing the fool? _____

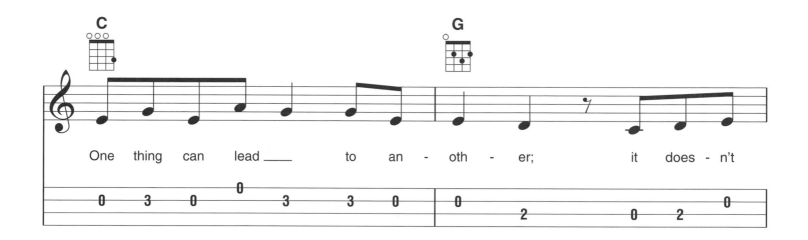

One thing can lead ____ to an - oth - er; it does - n't

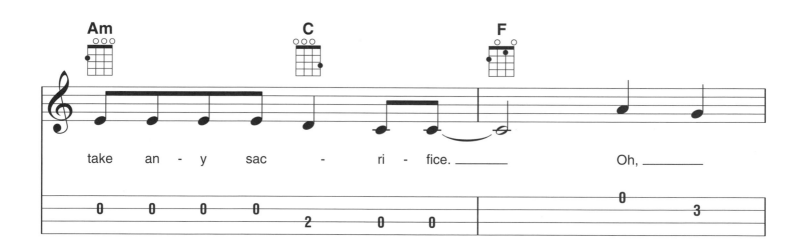

take an - y sac - ri - fice. _____ Oh, _____

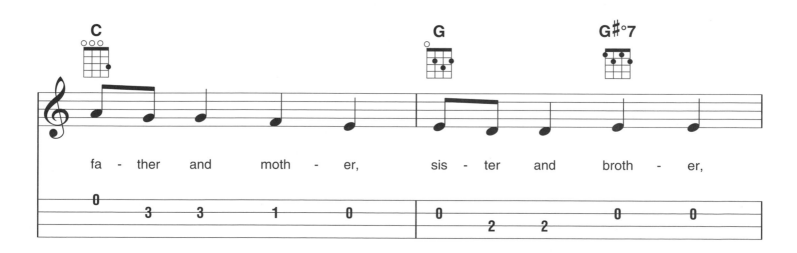

fa - ther and moth - er, sis - ter and broth - er,

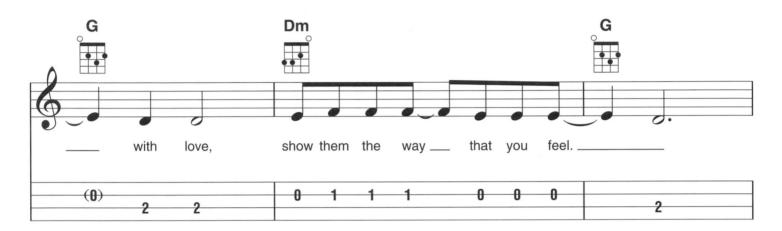

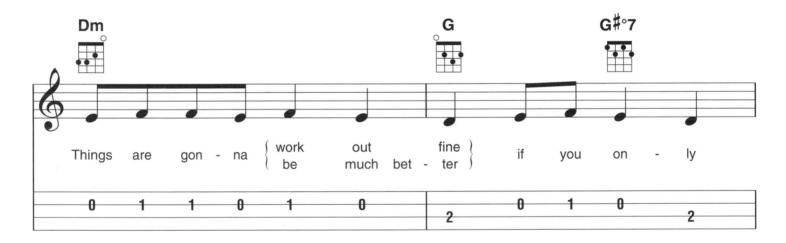

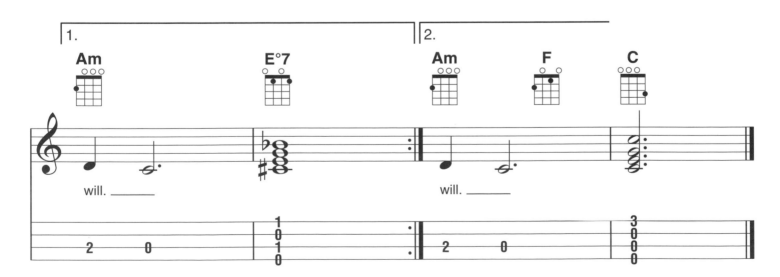

This page has been intentionally left blank to avoid an unnecessary page turn.

EVERY DAY I HAVE THE BLUES

Words and Music by
PETER CHATMAN

Verse

Shuffle feel

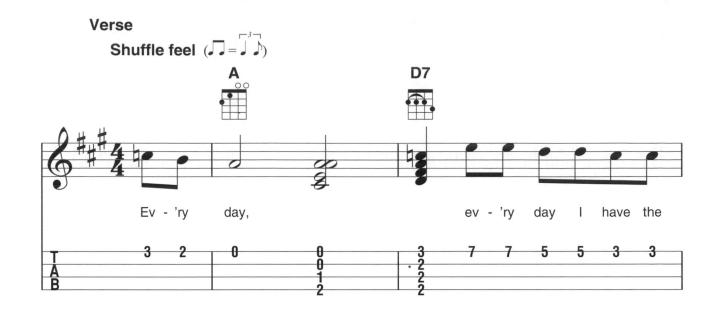

Ev - 'ry   day,   ev - 'ry day I have the

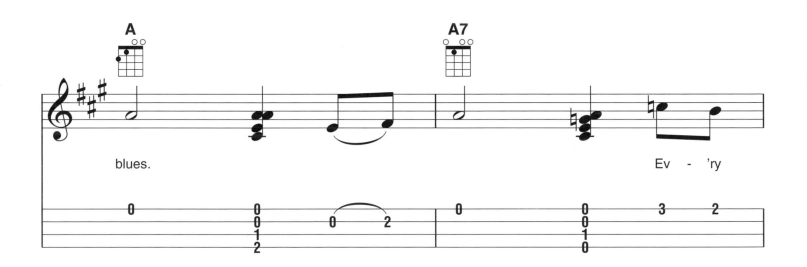

blues.   Ev - 'ry

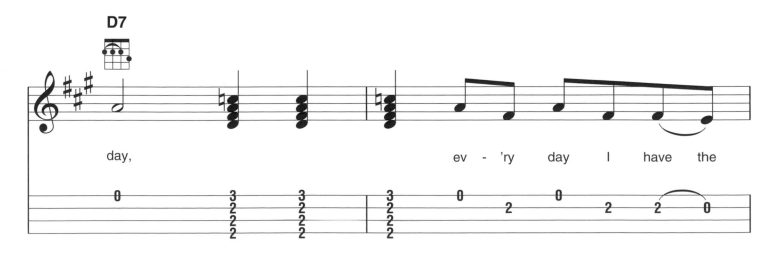

day,   ev - 'ry day I have the

blues.   Well, you

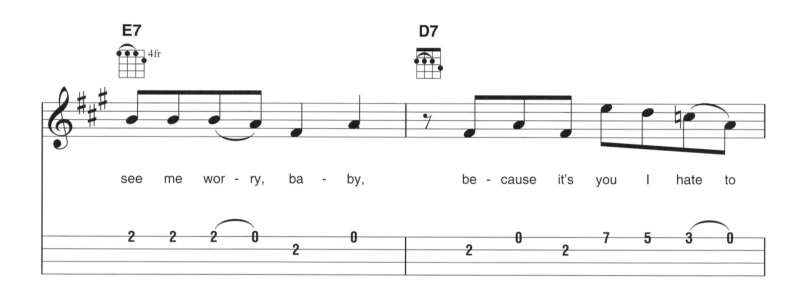

see me wor - ry, ba - by,   be - cause it's you I hate to

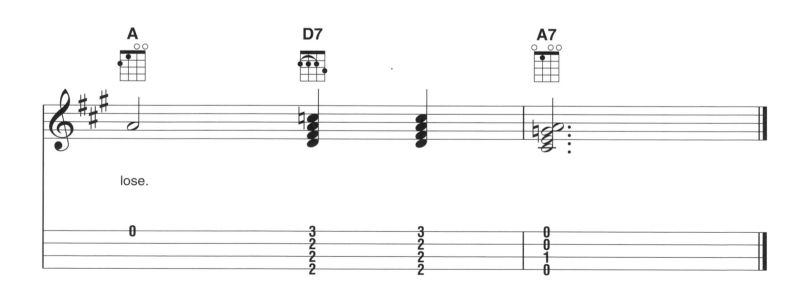

lose.

TAKE ME HOME, COUNTRY ROADS

Words and Music by JOHN DENVER,
BILL DANOFF and TAFFY NIVERT

TWIST AND SHOUT

Words and Music by BERT RUSSELL
and PHIL MEDLEY

ALICE'S RESTAURANT

Words and Music by
ARLO GUTHRIE

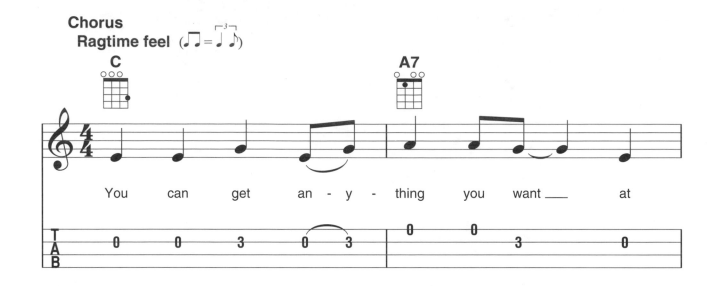

You can get an-y-thing you want ____ at

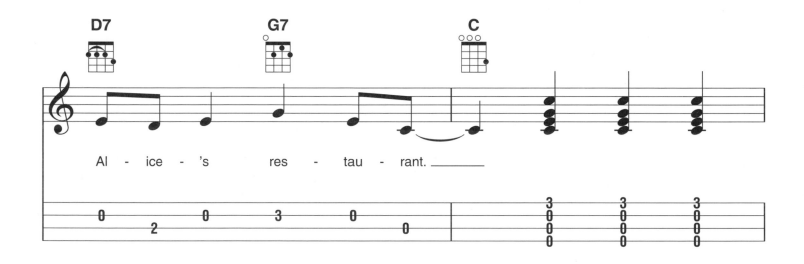

Al - ice -'s res - tau - rant. ____

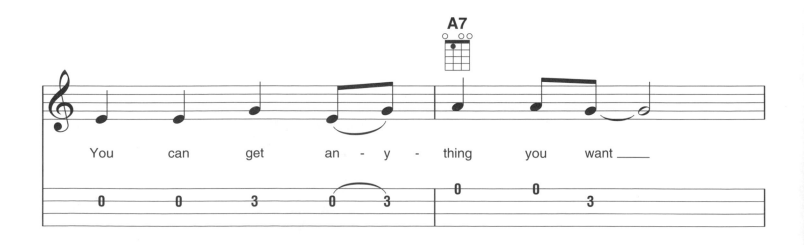

You can get an-y-thing you want ____

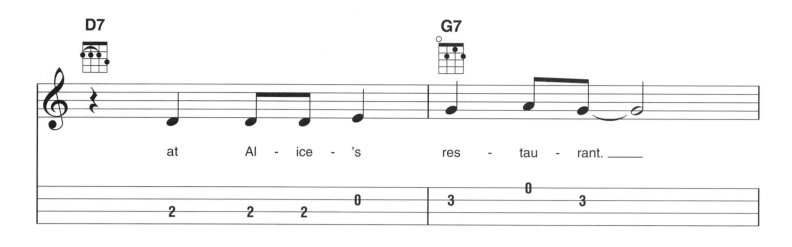

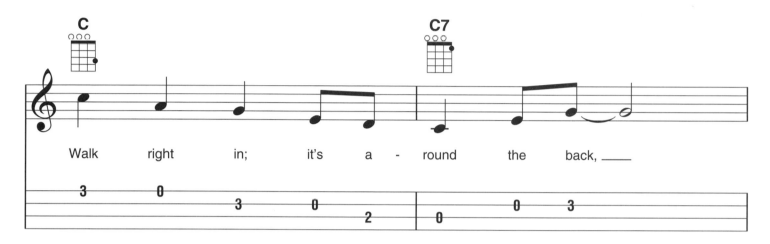

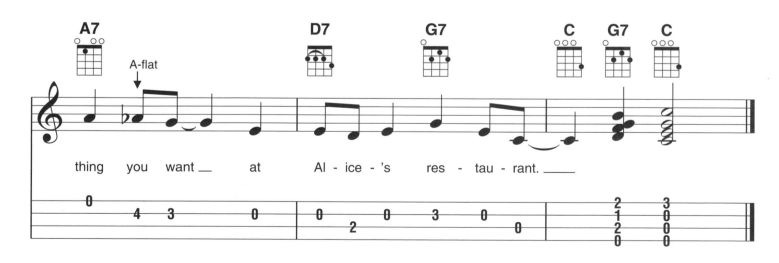

WALK RIGHT IN

Words and Music by GUS CANNON
and H. WOODS

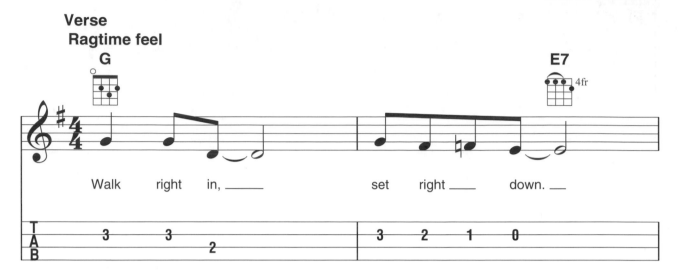

Walk right in, _____ set right _____ down. _____

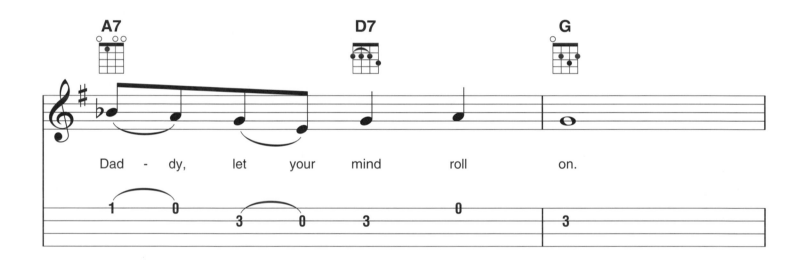

Dad - dy, let your mind roll on.

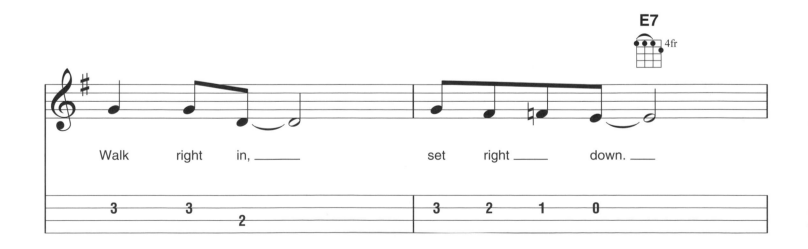

Walk right in, _____ set right _____ down. _____

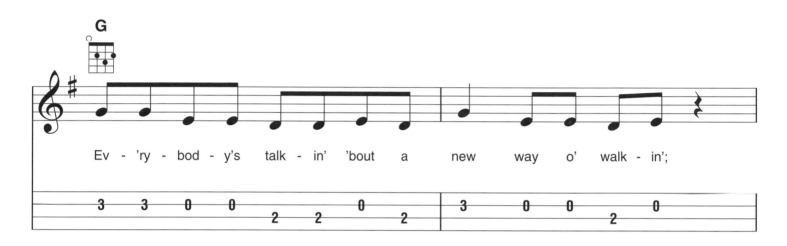

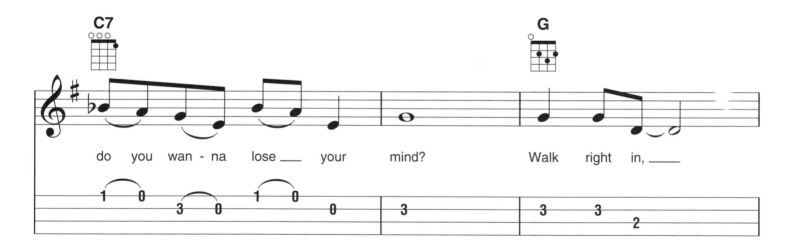

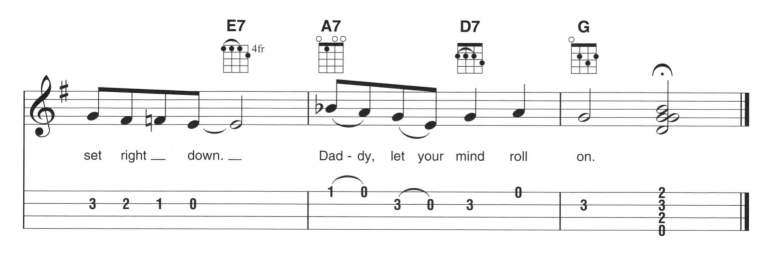

DO WAH DIDDY DIDDY

Words and Music by JEFF BARRY
and ELLIE GREENWICH

Verse
Calypso feel

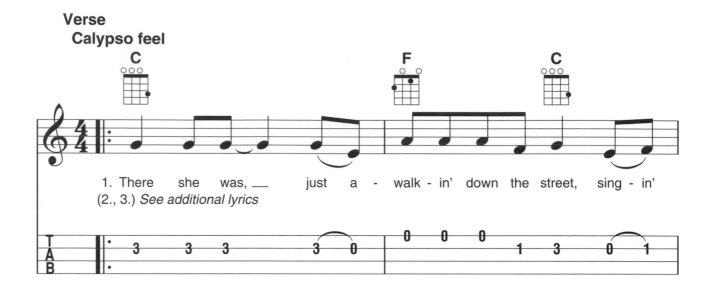

1. There she was, __ just a - walk - in' down the street, sing - in'
(2., 3.) *See additional lyrics*

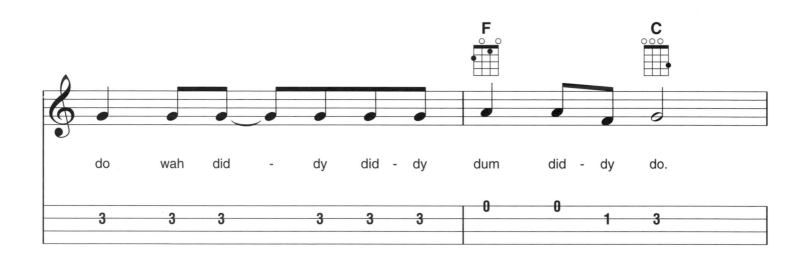

do wah did - dy did - dy dum did - dy do.

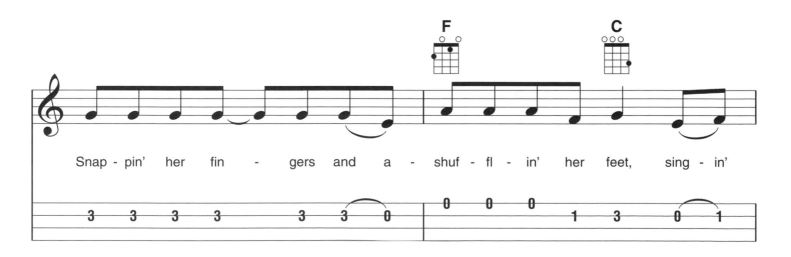

Snap - pin' her fin - gers and a - shuf - fl - in' her feet, sing - in'

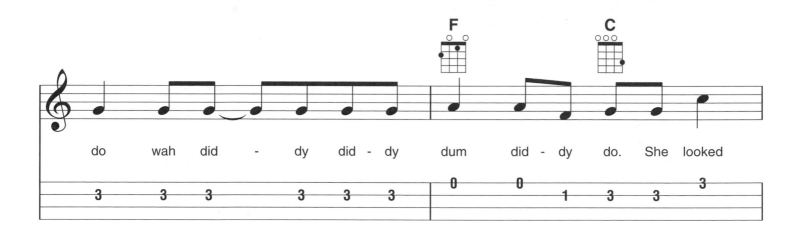

do wah did - dy did - dy dum did - dy do. She looked

To Coda ⊕

good (looked good), she looked fine (looked fine). She looked good, she looked fine, and I

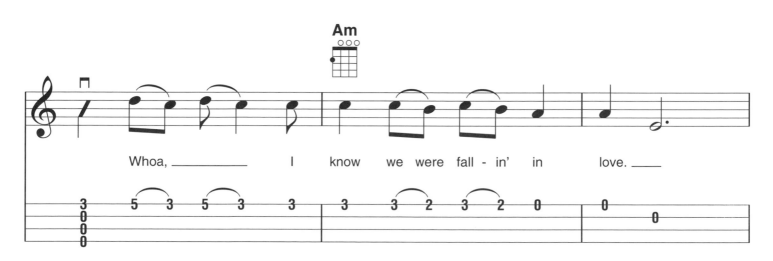

near-ly lost my mind. 2. Be - kissed a lit-tle more.

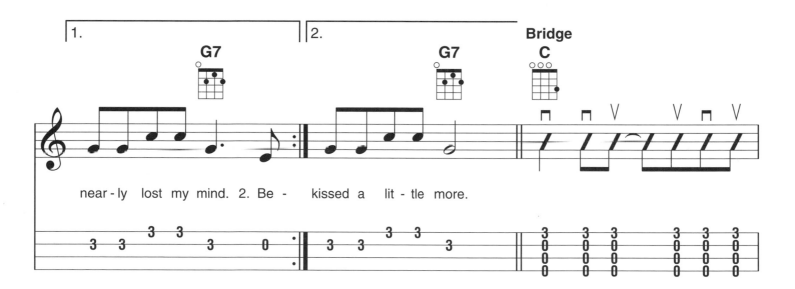

Whoa, _____ I know we were fall-in' in love. ____

Additional Lyrics

2. Before I knew it, she was walkin' next to me,
   Singin' do wah diddy diddy dum diddy do.
   Holdin' my hand just as natural as can be,
   Singin' do wah diddy diddy dum diddy do.
   We walked on (walked on) to my door (my door).
   We walked on to my door, then we kissed a little more.

3. Now we're together nearly ev'ry single day,
   Singin' do wah diddy diddy dum diddy do.
   We're so happy and that's how we're gonna stay,
   Singin' do wah diddy diddy dum diddy do.
   Well, I'm hers (I'm hers), she's mine (she's mine.)
   I'm hers, she's mine; wedding bells are gonna chime.

This page has been intentionally left blank to avoid an unnecessary page turn.

SWAY
(Quien Será)

English Words by NORMAN GIMBEL
Spanish Words and Music by
PABLO BELTRAN RUIZ

Verse
Calypso feel

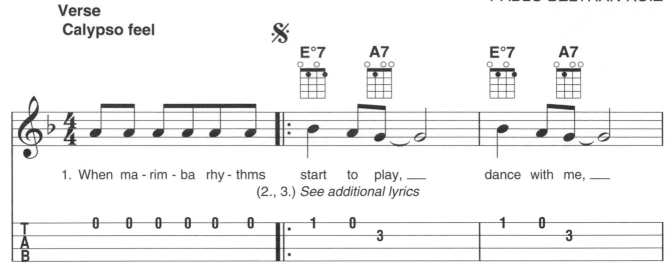

1. When ma-rim-ba rhy-thms start to play, ___ dance with me, ___
(2., 3.) *See additional lyrics*

make me sway. ___ Like the la-zy o-cean hugs the shore, ___

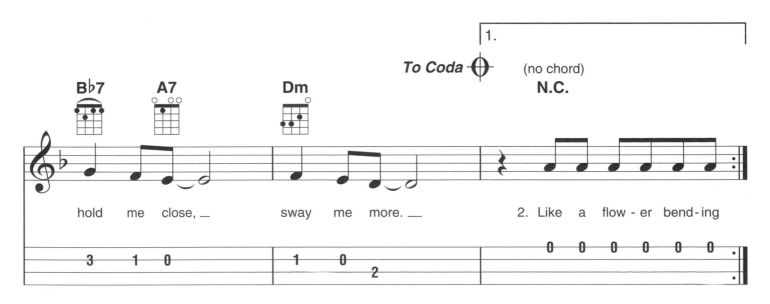

hold me close, ___ sway me more. ___ 2. Like a flow-er bend-ing

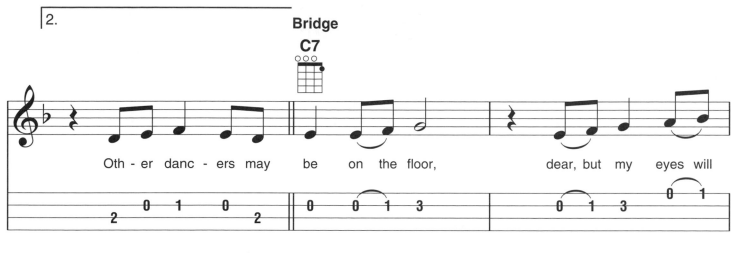

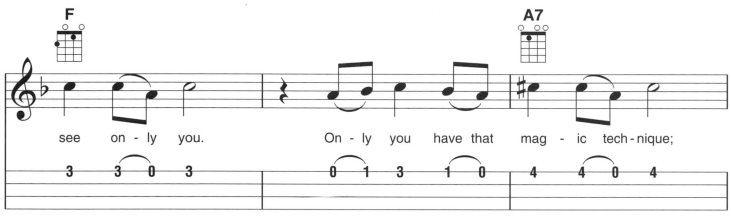

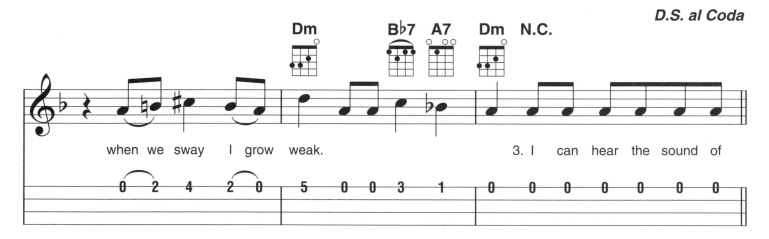

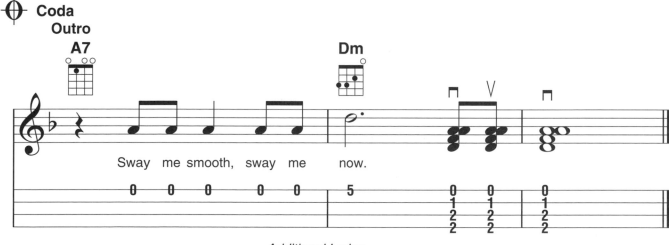

Additional Lyrics

2. Like a flower bending in the breeze,
   Bend with me, sway with ease.
   When we dance, you have a way with me.
   Stay with me, sway with me.

3. I can hear the sound of violins
   Long before it begins.
   Make me thrill as only you know how.
   Sway me smooth, sway me now.

HOUND DOG

Words and Music by JERRY LEIBER
and MIKE STOLLER

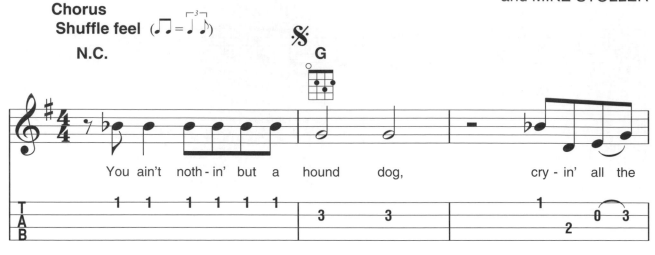

You ain't noth-in' but a hound dog, cry-in' all the

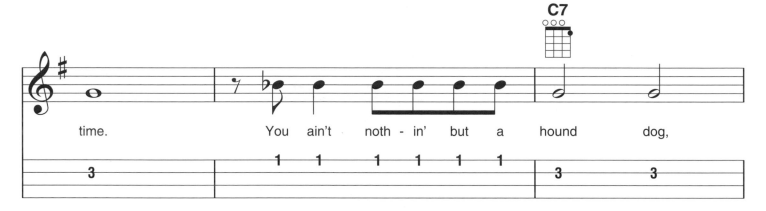

time. You ain't noth-in' but a hound dog,

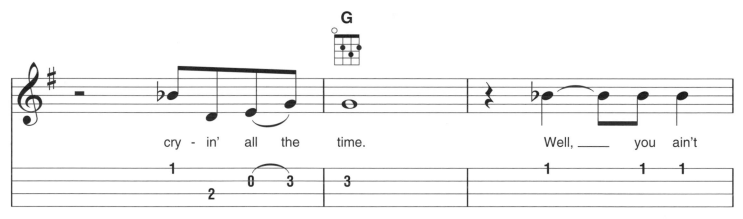

cry-in' all the time. Well, _____ you ain't

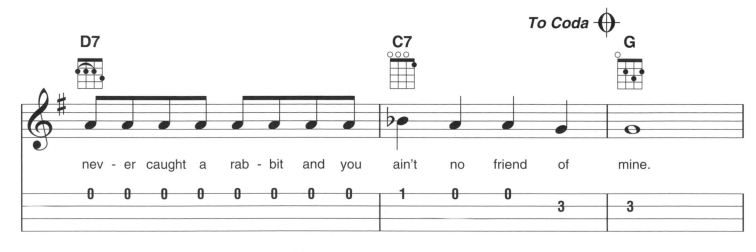

nev-er caught a rab-bit and you ain't no friend of mine.

ROCK AROUND THE CLOCK

Words and Music by MAX C. FREEDMAN
and JIMMY DeKNIGHT

38

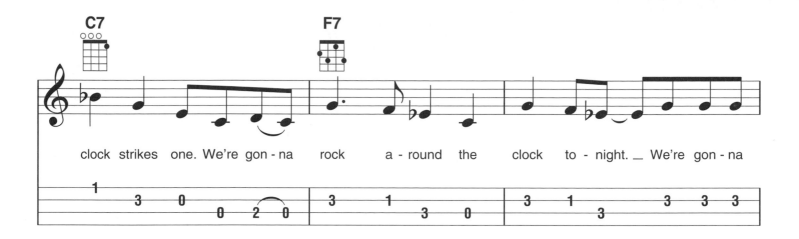

clock strikes one. We're gon - na rock a - round the clock to - night. __ We're gon - na

rock, rock, rock till broad day - light. __ We're gon - na rock, gon - na rock a -

Outro

round the clock __ to - night.

HALLELUJAH

Words and Music by
LEONARD COHEN

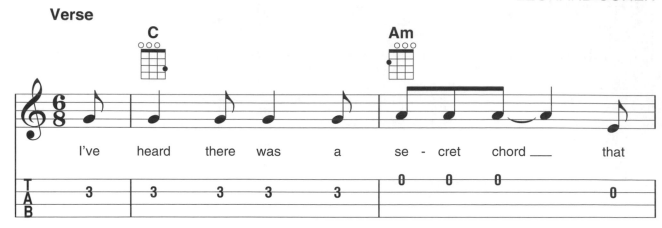

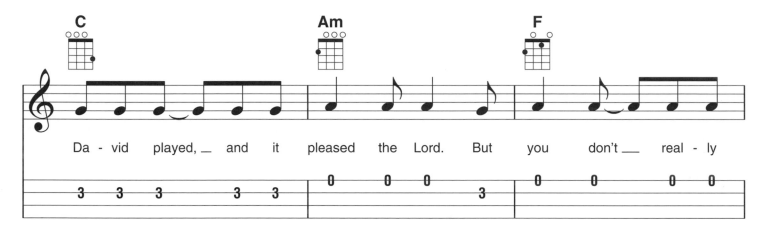

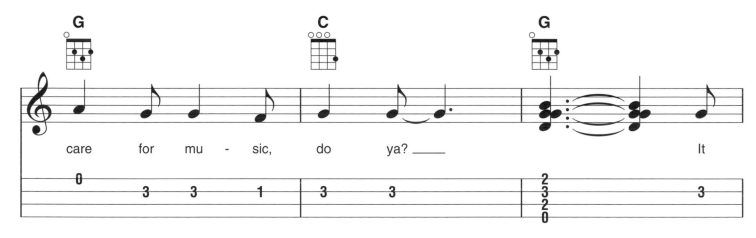

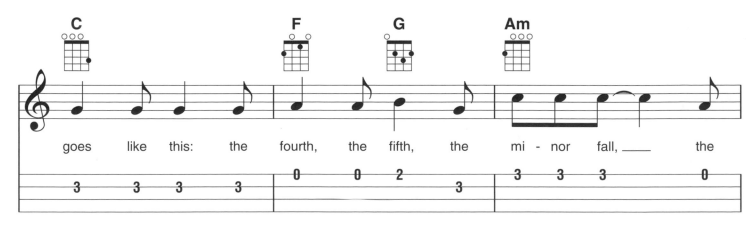

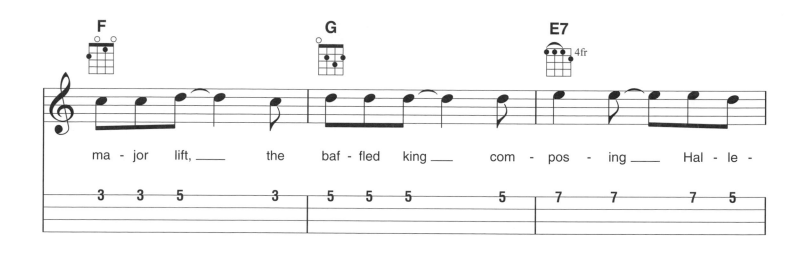

ma - jor lift, _____ the baf - fled king _____ com - pos - ing _____ Hal - le -

lu - jah. _____ Hal - le - lu - jah, Hal - le -

lu - jah, Hal - le - lu - jah, Hal - le -

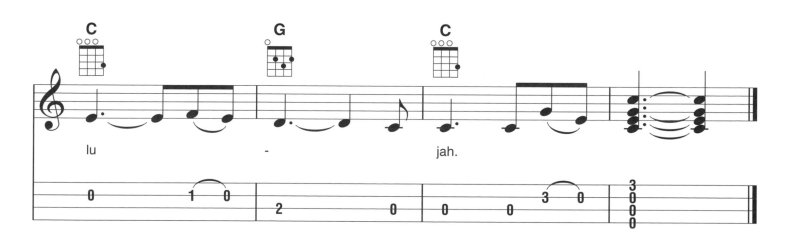

lu - jah.

WHEN I NEED YOU

Words and Music by CAROLE BAYER SAGER
and ALBERT HAMMOND

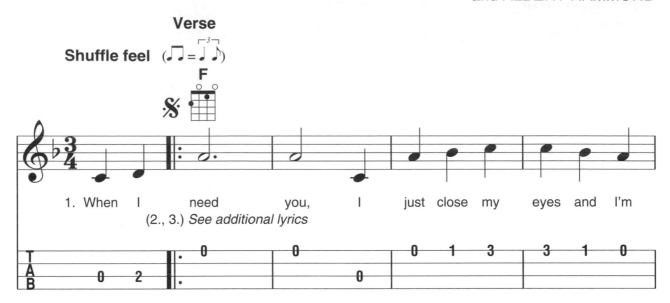

1. When I need you, I just close my eyes and I'm
(2., 3.) *See additional lyrics*

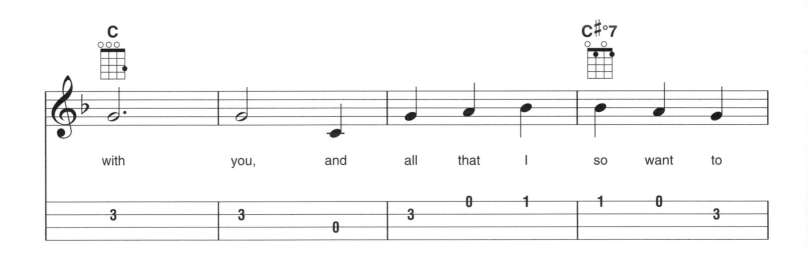

with you, and all that I so want to

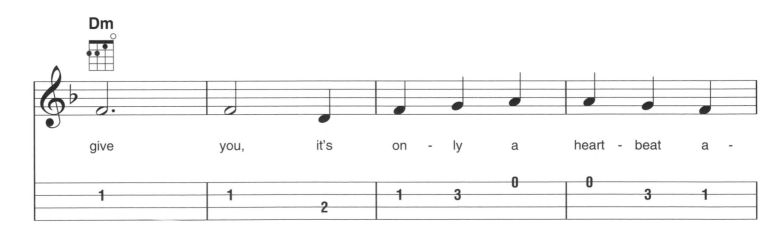

give you, it's on- ly a heart- beat a-

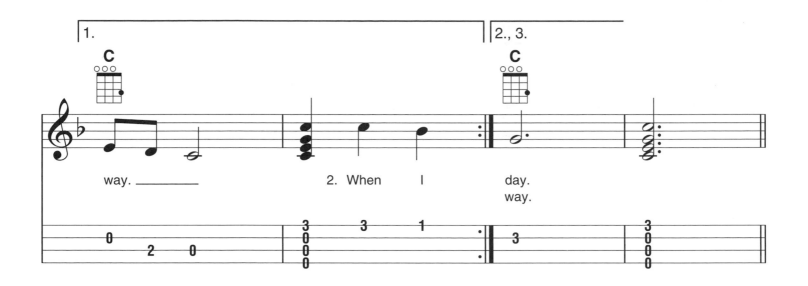

way. _____

2. When I day.
way.

Bridge

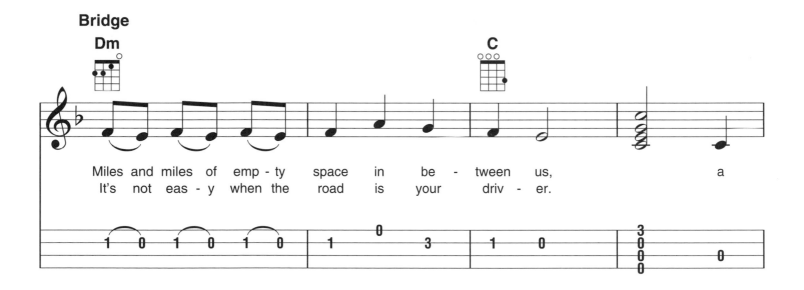

Miles and miles of emp-ty space in be-tween us, a
It's not eas-y when the road is your driv-er.

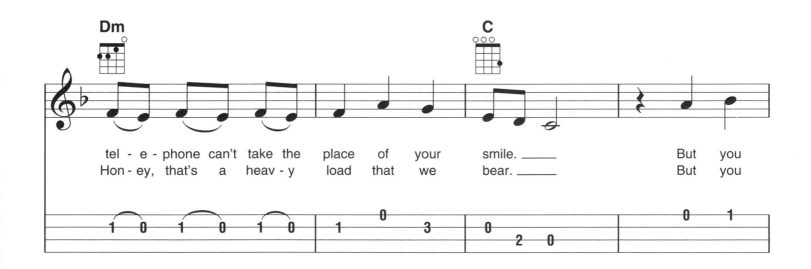

tel-e-phone can't take the place of your smile. _____ But you
Hon-ey, that's a heav-y load that we bear. _____ But you

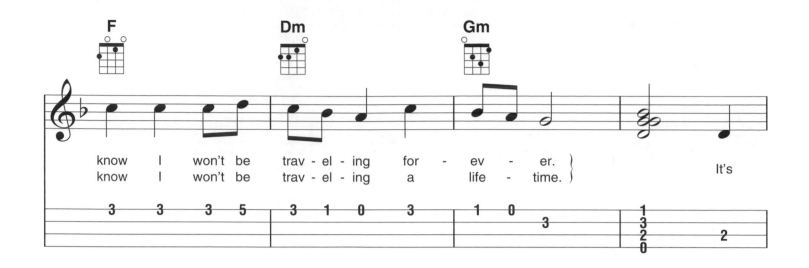

know   I   won't   be   trav - el - ing   for - ev - er.
know   I   won't   be   trav - el - ing   a   life - time.

It's

To Coda

D.S. al Coda
(take 2nd ending)

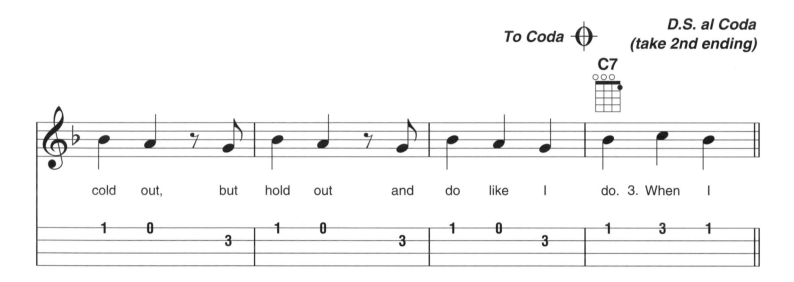

cold   out,   but   hold   out   and   do   like   I   do.   3. When   I

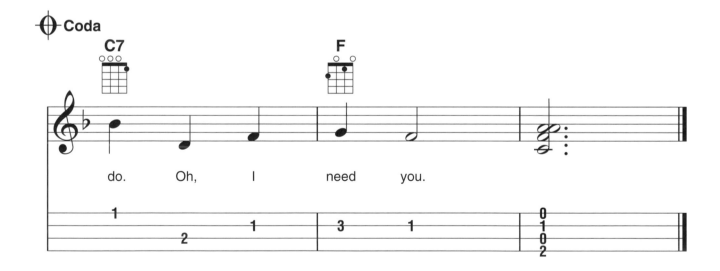

Coda

do.   Oh,   I   need   you.

Additional Lyrics

2. When I need love,
   I hold out my hands and I touch love.
   I never knew there was so much love
   Keeping me warm night and day.

3. When I need you,
   I just close my eyes and I'm with you,
   And all that I so want to give you, babe,
   It's only a heartbeat away.

NORWEGIAN WOOD
(This Bird Has Flown)

Words and Music by JOHN LENNON
and PAUL McCARTNEY

Verse

1. I once had a girl, or should I
2. *Instrumental*

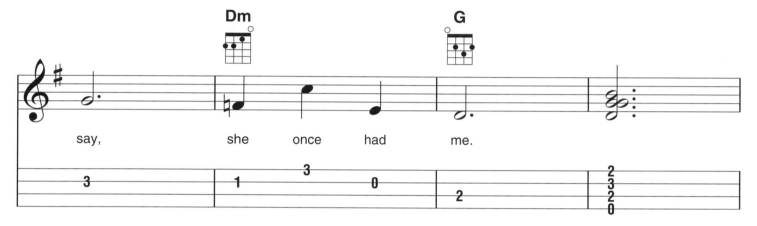

say, she once had me.

She showed me her room, is - n't it

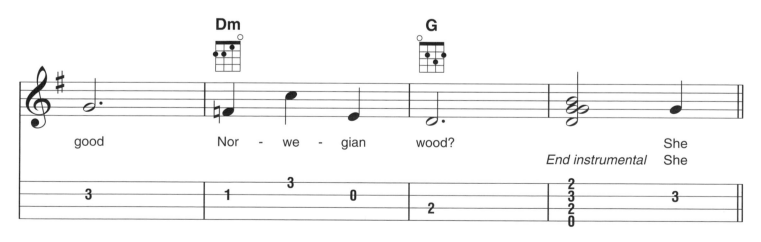

good Nor - we - gian wood?

End instrumental She She

Bridge

asked me to stay and she told me to sit an-y-
told me she worked in the morn-ing and start-ed to

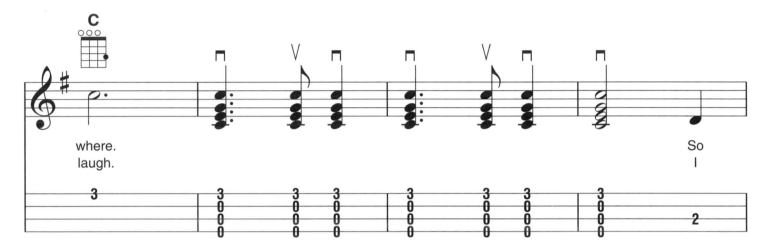

where.
laugh.
So I

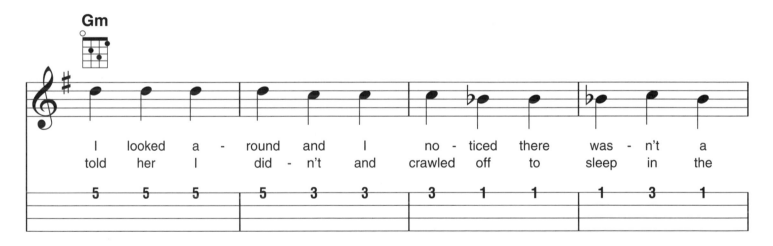

I looked a-round and I no-ticed there was-n't a
told her I did-n't and crawled off to sleep in the

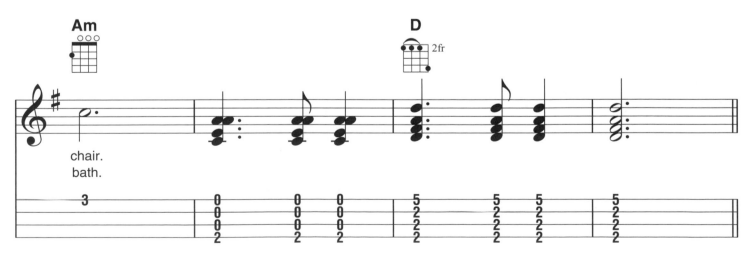

chair.
bath.

46

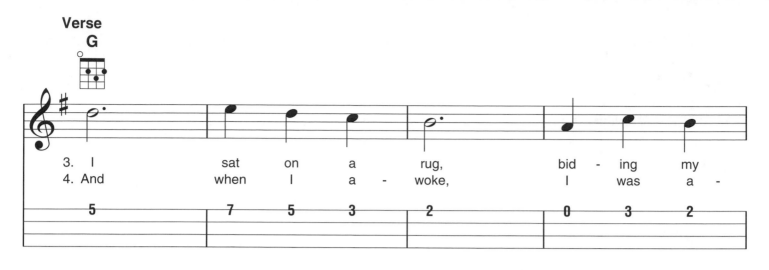

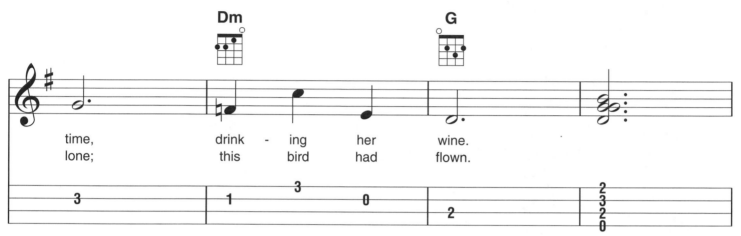

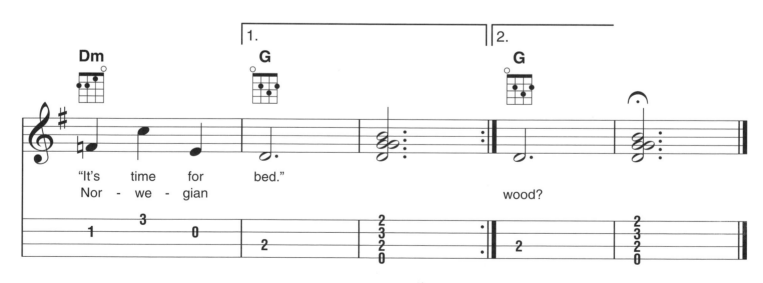

HAL•LEONARD® UKULELE PLAY-ALONG

AUDIO ACCESS INCLUDED

Now you can play your favorite songs on your uke with great-sounding backing tracks to help you sound like a bona fide pro! The audio also features playback tools so you can adjust the tempo without changing the pitch and loop challenging parts.

Prices, contents, and availability subject to change without notice.

HAL•LEONARD®

www.halleonard.com